comparative superlative

singular plural

FLASH FORWARD

Language Arts

figurative persuasive

Written by **Kathy Furgang**

Illustrations by **Jannie Ho**

Cover illustration by John Haslam
Cover design by Loira Walsh
Interior design by Gladys Lai
Production by Design Lab NYC, Inc.
Edited by Hilda Diaz

Flash Kids
A Division of Barnes & Noble
122 Fifth Avenue
New York, NY 10011

ISBN: 978-1-4114-2734-1

Please submit all inquiries to FlashKids@bn.com

Printed and bound in the United States

1 3 5 7 9 10 8 6 4 2

Communication, both written and oral, is vital to success in school.

Language Arts encompasses these essential skills. Through almost 100 pages of entertaining language exercises for sixth-graders, this workbook covers important topics such as reading comprehension, phonics, grammar, vocabulary, writing, and speaking.

Flash Forward Language Arts features mazes, puzzles, and activities designed to help your student develop grammar, spelling, and writing skills. Your student will learn to identify prefixes and suffixes, understand subject-verb agreement, separate fact and opinion, and distinguish between subject and object pronouns. This workbook also includes plenty of creative writing exercises and practice in numerous test-taking formats, including multiple-choice and open-ended questions.

The activities in this workbook are designed for your student to handle alone, but your assistance and interaction can greatly enhance the learning experience. As you work through the activities together, challenge your student to stretch his or her skills. Remember, however, that some concepts here will be new and require patience to master. Offer your student plenty of praise and support. After the completion of each page, you can check the answers at the back of the workbook. Use incorrect answers as an opportunity to review and rework.

In addition to working together on the pages of this book, you can encourage language skills through everyday activities. Here are some simple, age-appropriate ways to incorporate writing and oral skills into daily life. Ask your student to:

- Compare and contrast two characters from a favorite book
- Recount the sequence of events from a television show or movie
- Write a first-person narrative about an important event
- Proofread his or her own writings for proper grammar and punctuation
- Use graphic organizers and brainstorming to help write homework assignments
- Use context clues to identify unknown words in everyday reading

These and dozens of other activities are excellent ways to help your student develop essential communications skills. Remember, language is everywhere!

Do What's Proper!

A **common noun** names any person, place, or thing. A **proper noun** names a specific person, place, or thing. Use a capital letter to begin a proper noun.

For example:
Common nouns: holiday, soldier, museum, hardware store, street
Proper nouns: Valentine's Day, Major Rodriguez, Boston Children's Museum,
Barth's Hardware Store, Springfield Avenue

Rewrite each sentence correctly using capital letters for common and proper nouns.

1. Laura and Alexander went to the movies on jay street yesterday.

_____

2. Alexander could not believe his christmas holiday was almost over.

_____

3. He knew that it was almost time for aunt sarah to drive him to the albany airport.

_____

4. He missed his mom and dad back home, and he even missed his dog, tootsie.

_____

5. Next christmas break, alexander wants to visit washington, d.c., or austin, texas.

_____

6. He gets to choose where he visits each year with his cousin, laura.

_____

7. This year he went to laura's hometown to see her in a stage production of annie.

_____

8. Aunt sarah took them to dinner at millie's diner after the show.

_____

9. Alexander ordered eggnog because it was the december holiday.

_____

10. Eggnog reminds alexander of being at home in new hampshire.

_____

Prefixes All Around

A **prefix** is a word part that appears before a root word or base word. A prefix changes the meaning of the base word.

For example:
Post– is a prefix that means *after*, so the word *postseason* means *after the season*.

Rewrite each sentence. Replace the two underlined words with one word that uses a prefix.

1. Jackson will have to <u>organize</u> his bookshelf <u>again</u>.

_____

2. Dave is <u>not</u> <u>patient</u> and does not want to wait for his friend.

_____

3. The boys were supposed to <u>check</u> their math homework <u>again</u>.

_____

4. The time they spent in school studying had been <u>not</u> <u>helpful</u>.

_____

5. Any time for study is <u>not</u> <u>perfect</u> in some way, they thought.

_____

Write the meaning of each word.

6. unfulfilled _____

7. predestined _____

8. extraordinary _____

9. repossess _____

10. postscript _____

Super Suffixes

A **suffix** is a word part that appears after a root word or base word. A suffix changes the meaning of the base word.

For example:
–ist is a suffix that means *one who studies*. So, *scientist* means *one who studies science*.

Complete the word in each sentence by circling the correct suffix in parentheses.

1. Our class was filled with excite_____. (ful / ment)

2. We won the relay race because of our determin_____. (ation / ist)

3. We performed like profession_____ athletes. (al / er)

4. I was a bit fear_____ of running against Luke Warren from the other class. (ant / ful)

5. Luke has always been an excell_____ runner and everyone cheered for him. (ance / ent)

6. But this year, I was the one who won the competi_____. (tion / ence)

Write the word with a suffix that means the same as each definition shown.

7. person who studies philosophy _____

8. the process of developing _____

9. the act of agreeing _____

10. having no humor _____

Making Contractions

A **contraction** is a way to combine two words into one. An apostrophe takes the place of missing letters in the contraction.

For example:
she will = she'll   should not = shouldn't   we have = we've

Rewrite each sentence. Use a contraction to replace the underlined part.

1. The school election <u>should have</u> been today, but we had a fire drill.

_____

2. The classes <u>did not</u> follow the established rules of fire drill behavior.

_____

3. The principal says <u>she will</u> find the students who misbehaved and punish them.

_____

4. This <u>could have</u> been a real fire, and people <u>did not</u> take the exercise seriously.

_____

Write the words on the line that make up the underlined contractions.

5. "<u>They'll</u> tell us when <u>it's</u> our turn, but we have to be patient," I said.

_____

6. "<u>I'm</u> too excited," said Maddie. "<u>Let's</u> get this over with!"

_____

7. "<u>You'll</u> be disqualified if <u>you're</u> not listening to the judge," I reminded her.

_____

8. "<u>Wouldn't</u> that be just our luck," she said. "Alright, <u>we'll</u> behave."

_____

A Friendly Letter

A **friendly letter** is an informal letter to a friend or relative. It uses casual language in complete sentences and correct grammar. A friendly letter has an opening and a closing to tell to whom and from whom the letter is being sent.

Write a friendly letter to someone you know. Tell the person what you plan on doing this weekend. Use complete sentences and include an opening and closing.

_____

_____

_____

_____

_____

_____

_____

_____

_____

_____

_____

_____

_____

_____

How Can I Describe That?

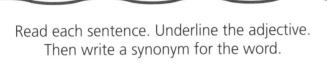

An **adjective** is a word that describes a noun or a pronoun.
Adjectives can explain *how many, how much, which,* and *what kind.*

For example:
My state is a *great* place to live.   (*great* describes <u>place</u>)

Read each sentence. Underline the adjective.
Then write a synonym for the word.

1. We have gorgeous areas of fields for growing crops.

   _____

2. I live on one of the smallest farms in the country.

   _____

3. We still need a powerful tractor to do the work, though.

   _____

4. At the end of the summer we have excess piles of corn.

   _____

5. Dad brings the most impressive goods to the farmer's market.

   _____

6. This is one of the most important ways that our family makes money.

   _____

7. My eager sister helps sell the corn at our booth at the market.

   _____

8. I stay home and prepare next week's supplies for a successful trip into town.

   _____

What's the Subject?

The **subject** of a sentence is what the sentence is about. When a sentence is a question, change it into a statement so you can easily find the subject. When the sentence is a command, change it into a statement to find the subject.

For example:
Question: Are you coming with us?   **Statement:** You should come with us.
Command: Hurry up!   **Statement:** You should hurry up.
The subject of both sentences is *you*.

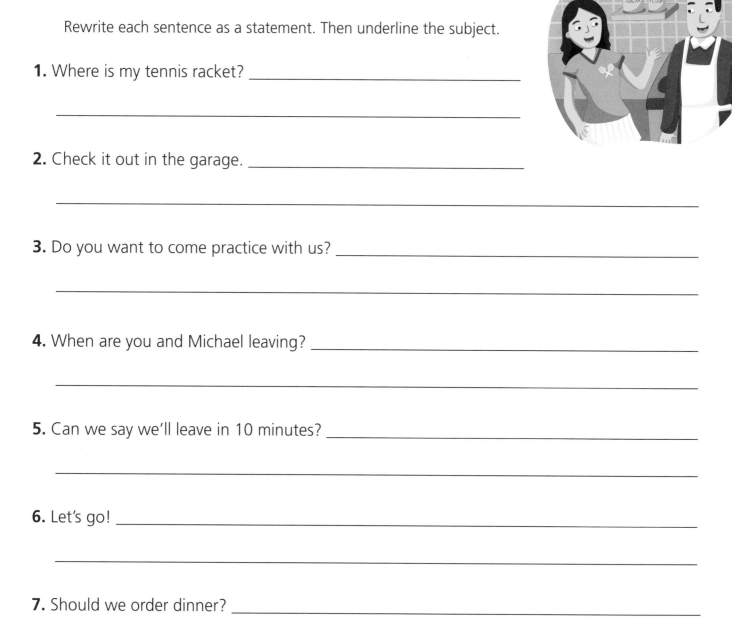

Rewrite each sentence as a statement. Then underline the subject.

1. Where is my tennis racket? _____

_____

2. Check it out in the garage. _____

_____

3. Do you want to come practice with us? _____

_____

4. When are you and Michael leaving? _____

_____

5. Can we say we'll leave in 10 minutes? _____

_____

6. Let's go! _____

_____

7. Should we order dinner? _____

_____

So Few and So Many

A **singular noun** names one person, place, or thing. A **plural noun** names more than one person, place, or thing. To make a plural noun, an *–s* or an *–es* is added to the end of a singular noun. Sometimes, singular and plural nouns look and sound the same. Other times, the words are completely different.

For example:
Singular nouns: alligator, fox, deer, moose, mouse, goose
Plural nouns: alligators, foxes, deer, moose, mice, geese

Read each sentence. Underline each singular noun. Circle each plural noun.

1. Andrew mowed the lawn and raked the leaves.

2. The man who lives across the street has two dogs.

3. He takes them for a walk without their leashes.

4. Neighbors up and down the block complain.

5. "Get those dogs off my lawn!" they say.

Complete each sentence with the plural noun form of the word in parentheses.

6. We were the best _____ at the assembly today. (child)

7. Gabby complained a little because she had two loose _____. (tooth)

8. There were two giant _____ on the stage that blocked our view. (cactus)

9. Afterwards, we shared our snacks by cutting the sandwiches into _____. (half)

10. It was one of the best afternoons of our _____. (life)

Looking Good!

Descriptive writing gives details about something. Descriptions help to make writing more exact and interesting for the reader. They paint a picture in the reader's mind.

Choose a piece of clothing from your dresser drawer at home.
Examine it carefully and write a detailed description of it.

Prefix Party

> Remember: A **prefix** is a word part that appears before a root word or a base word. A prefix changes the meaning of the original word.

Complete the chart with a word that uses that prefix.

Prefix	Meaning	Word
1. pre-	before	
2. post-	after	
3. un-	not	
4. over-	too much	
5. im-	not	
6. ex-	out	

Read each sentence. Underline the word that is formed with a prefix. Then write the meaning of the word.

7. Her coach may be inexperienced, but she is well liked among her athletes.

_____

8. Some leaders lack interpersonal skills, while others lack knowledge.

_____

9. The coach may be overemphasizing hitting when we need more work on catching.

_____

10. We may have to reschedule Saturday's game if it rains.

_____

Superb Suffixes

Remember: A **suffix** is a word part that appears after a root word or a base word. A suffix changes the meaning of the root or base word.

Complete the chart with a word that uses that suffix.

Suffix	Meaning	Word
1. -ing	in the process of	
2. -able	capable of	
3. -ful	full of	
4. -ation, -tion	action or process	
5. -ism	belief, or set of principles	
6. -ist, -or	one who	

Read each sentence. Underline the word that is formed with a suffix.
Then write the meaning of the word.

7. Jessie dreams of being in the car races one day, but Tommy says he is doubtful it will happen.

_____

8. "You don't have what it takes to be a professional," said Tommy.

_____

9. "Well, that's very rude," said Jessie calmly.

_____

10. "Just kidding," laughed Tommy. "No one has as much determination as you do."

_____

Synonym and Antonym Shuffle

Synonyms are words that mean the same or almost the same as other words.
Antonyms are words that have opposite meanings.

For example:
Synonyms: devoted/loyal   huge/gigantic   great/super
Antonyms: evil/kind   fascinating/dull   diligent/lazy

Replace the underlined word in each sentence with a synonym.
Write the word on the line.

1. Marcus was <u>disappointed</u> with his meal. _____

2. He thought the food looked <u>beautiful</u> on the plate. _____

3. The mashed potatoes were cold and the meat was <u>tough</u>. _____

Replace the underlined word in each sentence with an antonym.
Write the word on the line.

4. Jen is going to her <u>last</u> babysitting job of the year.

_____

5. The Baxter twins always acted <u>horribly</u>.

_____

6. She always thought babysitting them was <u>difficult</u>.

_____

Complete the chart. Write a synonym and an antonym for each word.

Word	Synonym	Antonym
7. bashful		
8. creative		
9. delicious		
10. friendly		

Feeling Tense?

A verb's **tense** tells when action takes place. The **past tense** tells about actions that have already taken place. The **present tense** tells about actions that are happening now. The **future tense** tells about actions that have not yet taken place.

For example:
Past tense: Caleb *tried* to blow up the balloon.
Present tense: Caleb *tries* to blow up the balloon.
Future tense: Caleb *will try* to blow up the balloon.

Read each sentence. What tense is it written in? Write *past, present*, or *future*.

1. Sonal made cookies for her birthday party. _____

2. The guests will be here any minute. _____

3. Sonal is still getting ready in the bathroom. _____

Write a sentence that uses the verb in the tense shown.

4. greet (present)

_____

5. smile (future)

_____

6. forgive (past)

_____

Rewrite each sentence in the future tense.

7. Each guest puts his or her gift on the table.

_____

8. The kids play party games and eat snacks.

_____

9. Parents pick up their children at 3:00 PM sharp.

_____

Just the Facts

When a writer **prewrites**, he or she records important information. One way to prewrite is to record *who, what, when, where,* and *why* about a topic.

For example:
Who: Mae Jemison   **What:** first African-American woman in space
When: September 12, 1992   **Where:** Space Shuttle *Endeavor*
Why: to further her career as an astronaut and to make American history

Choose a person you would like to research and write about. Complete the chart with the information about the person. Then use the information to write a paragraph about the person.

Who	_____
What	_____
When	_____
Where	_____
Why	_____

_____

_____

_____

_____

_____

_____

_____

_____

Write First, Think Later

A **draft** is an important part of the writing process. A draft is a first attempt at a writing project. It is meant to get the writer's ideas down on paper and to help the writer think about the final draft. Drafts may have many errors that can be fixed in the final draft.

For example:

Draft: The fall leafs fell like rain thru the air. and Jason looked forward jumping in a pile of them.

Final copy: The fall leaves fell like rain through the air, and Jason looked forward to raking together a pile of them and jumping in!

Write a short draft about your favorite music. Do not worry about the exact wording or correct punctuation or spelling. Then rewrite the paragraph as a final copy.

Draft _____

_____

_____

_____

_____

_____

_____

Final copy _____

_____

_____

_____

_____

_____

_____

Titles and More Titles

When writing the **titles** of books, magazines, newspapers, TV shows, and movies, use italics. For the titles of songs, articles, stories, poems, or essays use quotation marks. Capitalize all important words of a title, including the first and last words.

For example:
"The Three Little Pigs" (story)   *Toy Story* (movie)
The Springfield Times (newspaper)   "Jack and Jill" (poem)

The titles below are all written incorrectly. Rewrite the titles correctly.

1. "mrs. frisby and the rats of nimh" (book) _____

2. "the wall street journal"(newspaper) _____

3. "Dancing with the Stars" (TV show) _____

4. *The Itsy-Bitsy Spider* (poem) _____

5. Star Wars (movie) _____

6. "the philadelphia inquirer" (newspaper) _____

7. "how-to make the best enchilada" (essay) _____

8. "Harry Potter and the Deathly Hallows" (book)

_____

9. *Helping at the main street soup kitchen* (article)

_____

10. "Sports Illustrated for Kids" (magazine)

_____

Compare and Contrast the Facts

When reading a nonfiction passage, it helps to **compare and contrast** the facts. Comparing means telling how things are similar. Contrasting means telling how things are different.

For example:
Similarity: Both baseball and football are played professionally in America.
Difference: A score in baseball is a home run; a score in football is a touchdown.

Read the passage and answer the questions below.

Children's book author E.B. White was born July 11, 1899, as Elwyn Brooks White. He graduated from Cornell University in 1921 and spent several years writing for magazines and newspapers. Then in the late 1930s he began writing children's books for his niece. *Stuart Little*, his first children's book, was published in 1945. His second, *Charlotte's Web*, was published in 1952. The public was slow to accept White's work, but he then began receiving awards for his work in the 1970s.

Children's book author J.K. Rowling was born July 31, 1965, as Joanne Rowling. Her first book in the *Harry Potter* series was published in the United States in 1998 under the name *Harry Potter and the Sorcerer's Stone*. Rowling's editor did not think young boys would be interested in reading a novel written by a woman, so Rowling decided to use initials. Since she does not have a middle name, she picked the middle initial *K* for Kathleen. There are a total of seven books in the *Harry Potter* series, and each book was extremely popular as soon as it was published.

1. Name four ways E.B. White and J.K. Rowling are alike.

_____

_____

_____

_____

2. Name four ways E.B. White and J.K. Rowling are different.

_____

_____

_____

_____

Name That Antecedent

An **antecedent** is a noun or group of nouns that a pronoun refers to. A pronoun must agree with its antecedent in number and gender.

For example:
Antecedent: <u>Leo's Sweet Shop and Meg's Dry Cleaners</u> are closed Thursday.
Pronoun: <u>They</u> are closed today.

Complete each sentence with the correct pronoun. Then underline the antecedent.

1. "Thursday is a big day," said Tori. "_____ is Thanksgiving."

2. "On holidays, the storekeepers take the day off. _____ spend the day with their families," said Tori.

3. "Your mom will have to think ahead about what she needs to buy. _____ has to shop ahead of time," I said.

4. "I know she needs a turkey, stuffing, and gravy," said Tori. "_____ are the things everyone needs at Thanksgiving."

5. "My family is not traditional on Thanksgiving," I told her. "_____ eat rice, beans, and tortillas."

6. "Yum!" said Tori. "May I come to your house with my sister on Thanksgiving? _____ really love tortillas!"

7. "Of course," I said. "But don't forget to bring me some stuffing from your house! Your mom is a great cook. _____ can cook for me any time."

8. "OK. I will let my sister know. _____ will be there around 7:00 PM."

Use Those Adjectives!

Descriptive adjectives help give the reader the most useful information about a topic. When writing, think about words that will best describe what you are writing about.

For example:
Mom's *blue and white striped* apron was *stained with spaghetti sauce* and *tattered at the neck* where it hung from the metal hook on the wall.

Think about your favorite food. Write a descriptive paragraph to describe it. Use as many adjectives as possible.

_____

_____

_____

_____

_____

_____

_____

_____

_____

_____

_____

_____

_____

Subject and Verb Agreement

The subject and verb of a sentence must be in **agreement**. Singular verbs are used with singular subjects. Plural verbs are used with plural subjects.

For example:
Singular: <u>Marcos buys</u> apples from the green market.
Plural: <u>His sisters bake</u> the best apple pie in the world.

Complete each sentence. Circle the correct verb in parentheses to agree with the subject of the sentence.

1. My friend (reply / replies) that he will go to the holiday party.

2. I (wish / wishes) he would pick me up on his way there.

3. I (have / has) no way to get to the party.

4. If my mom (change / changes) her work schedule that night, she can drive me.

Rewrite the paragraph below so that it uses correct subject-verb agreement.

5. My dog are the silliest dog on my street. Whenever we goes for a walk, he bark at the third house on the right, number 32. There are never anyone outside the house when he bark, and there usually isn't even any cars in the driveway. But he bark and bark until we passes it and it's far out of our sight. Maybe next time we will walks the other way to avoids this problem.

_____

_____

_____

_____

_____

_____

_____

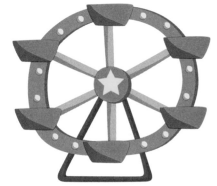

Super Sequencing

Sequencing means ordering information by time order, size order, or sequential order. You can sequence events in a fiction story or real events or steps in a nonfiction passage. Words such as *next*, *then*, *after*, and *finally* are clues about sequence.

Read the passage and answer the questions below.

The Quaker Falls town picnic is today. The participants in this year's games will be able to sign up ahead of time to make sure they are included in all of the games and events they wish to take part in. After the games, we will have a grilling contest. The person who makes the spiciest spare ribs wins a blue ribbon and a free ride on the Ferris wheel. The final events of the picnic include talent contests. There will be volunteer judges in the areas of singing, dancing, and comedy routines. After the last event, there will be a special drawing to see who will bring home the raffle ticket money. There will be plenty to do at the Quaker Falls town picnic!

1. What is the first event at the picnic?

_____

2. What happens at the event right before the talent contests?

_____

3. What is the last thing that happens at the picnic?

_____

4. Make a numbered list to show the schedule of the picnic events.

_____

_____

_____

_____

_____

_____

_____

Playing Around with Pronouns

A **subject pronoun** replaces a subject in a sentence. Subject pronouns are *I, you, they, we, he, she,* and *it*. **Object pronouns** replace objects in a sentence. Object pronouns are *me, us, them, you, her, him,* and *it*.

For example:
Subject pronoun: *We* are making pizza for dinner tonight.
Object pronoun: Should we save a slice for *you*?

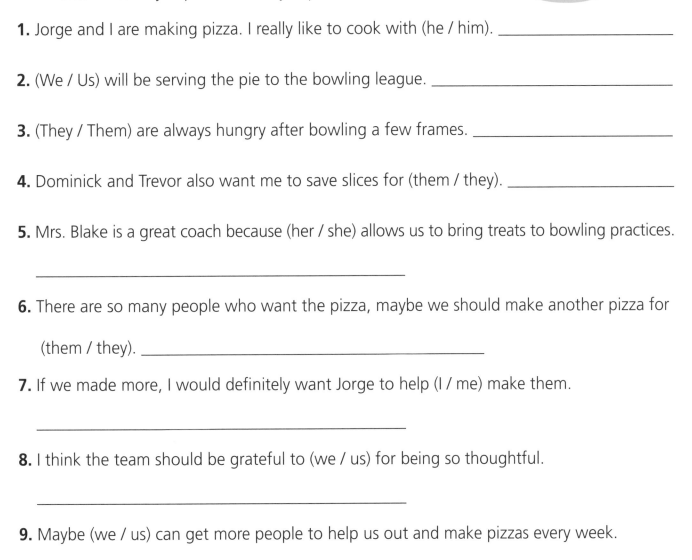

Complete each sentence. Circle the correct pronoun in parentheses.
Then write *subject pronoun* or *object pronoun* on the line.

1. Jorge and I are making pizza. I really like to cook with (he / him). _____

2. (We / Us) will be serving the pie to the bowling league. _____

3. (They / Them) are always hungry after bowling a few frames. _____

4. Dominick and Trevor also want me to save slices for (them / they). _____

5. Mrs. Blake is a great coach because (her / she) allows us to bring treats to bowling practices.

_____

6. There are so many people who want the pizza, maybe we should make another pizza for

(them / they). _____

7. If we made more, I would definitely want Jorge to help (I / me) make them.

_____

8. I think the team should be grateful to (we / us) for being so thoughtful.

_____

9. Maybe (we / us) can get more people to help us out and make pizzas every week.

_____

Punctuation Perfection

Punctuation marks make sentences sound clear to the reader and separate different parts of a sentence. Periods, commas, question marks, exclamation marks, quotation marks, and parentheses are all kinds of punctuation.

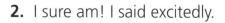

Rewrite each sentence using correct punctuation.

1. My mom doesnt think Im old enough to be a babysitter

_____

2. I sure am! I said excitedly.

_____

3. I used to take care of many babies in our neighborhood I reminded her.

_____

4. Everyone can use a little spare change and I think I could use some babysitting money to use when I go to the movies with my friends. Wouldn't you agree.

_____

_____

5. There is a girl down the street named whitney who is easy to babysit for

_____

6. "Would you like to come meet her with me I asked Mom.

_____

7. Well said Mom, maybe its not such a bad idea after all if you start babysitting

_____

Nifty Negatives!

Sentences that use words such as *never, nothing, no, nobody, nowhere,* and *not* use a **negative** expression. With a **double negative**, two negatives are used in the same sentence. Double negatives are incorrect because they change the meaning of the sentence to have a positive meaning.

For example:
Correct: Dawn does not have anywhere to go.
Double negative: Dawn does not have nowhere to go.
Meaning: Dawn has somewhere to go.

Rewrite each sentence so that it does not have a double negative.
Keep only the first negative in each sentence.

1. Pam does not want nobody to get hurt on the new playground.

_____

2. She won't not let the crews put up swing sets that are dangerous.

_____

3. Nothing won't stop her from doing the job right.

_____

4. An unsafe playground isn't fun for nobody.

_____

5. The workers will draw a line in front of the swings so no one won't get hit.

_____

6. Better grip handles will be put on the monkey bars so little hands won't never slip.

_____

7. There won't be nowhere in town with such a safe playground.

_____

A Good Description!

An **adjective phrase** is a prepositional phrase that describes a noun or pronoun. Adjective phrases tell about how many or what kind of noun or pronoun they are describing.

For example:
Thousands *of roses* covered the parade float. (describes <u>thousands</u>)
The coach *with the green hat* is ours. (describes <u>coach</u>)
The party *after the parade* is going to be fun. (describes <u>party</u>)

Read each sentence. Underline the adjective phrase. Circle the word that the phrase describes.

1. I am wearing a raincoat with a hood because the weather report calls for rain.

2. Jackie saw a line of fifty people waiting to get into the parade area.

3. This will be a parade of great importance for our baseball league.

4. Players from every team will be here.

5. We're celebrating the teams with the best sportsmanship.

6. Everyone in the parade should be proud.

7. My dad will be one of the people on the sidelines.

8. My mom will be one of the volunteers in the float.

9. I have a whole family of great supporters.

Off to a Good Start

The **beginning** of a story introduces the characters and main events. A story's beginning might also introduce the story's conflict, or problem. Story beginnings should be as interesting as possible to catch the reader's attention.

Write a beginning for the story ending below.

_____

_____

_____

_____

_____

_____

_____

_____

_____

_____

_____

_____

_____

_____

_____

    The boys ran back from the field cheering and jumping for joy. They only had one more game until the championship, and they finally had their star player back, healthy and ready to play. They knew the next game would go much more smoothly than this one did.

It's a Pronoun. . . Indefinitely!

> An **indefinite pronoun** is a pronoun that doesn't refer to a specific thing, person, or place. Words like *everyone, everything, anybody, most, many*, and *few* are examples of indefinite pronouns. *Singular* indefinite pronouns must use singular verbs in a sentence. *Plural* indefinite pronouns must use plural verbs in a sentence.
>
> For example:
> **Singular indefinite pronoun:** *Everybody* likes my sneakers.
> **Plural indefinite pronoun:** *All* of the people like my socks.

Read each sentence. Underline the indefinite pronoun. Then write *singular* or *plural*.

1. Some of my friends are leaving now. _____

2. Many of them are late for a picnic. _____

3. Nobody can start a picnic without me! _____

4. Everybody poses for a picture at the picnic. _____

5. Few of the people eat the watermelon. _____

Complete each sentence by circling the correct verb in parentheses.

6. Someone (ring / rings) the doorbell on Saturday afternoon.

7. Mom says nobody (come / comes) in the house while she is gone.

8. Some of my friends (want / wants) to play.

9. "Nobody (is / are) home with me," I tell them.

10. Everyone (sigh / sighs) and walks away.

I'm in Agreement!

Subject-verb agreement means that the subject of a sentence agrees in number with the verb of the sentence. A plural subject uses a plural verb. A singular subject uses a singular verb.

For example:
I wash my uniform before practice.
The coaches compliment us on our good performance.

Complete each sentence by circling the correct form of each verb in parentheses to agree with the subject.

1. A new bookstore (open / opens) on Main Street tomorrow.

2. I (want / wants) to go there to see what books they have.

3. The books in the store (look / looks) like they are stacked to the ceiling.

4. Sometimes I cannot (reach / reaches) the high shelves.

5. The customers must (want / wants) a large selection of books to choose from.

6. Visitors (like / likes) the look of the new store when they peek in the window.

7. People (see / sees) computers sitting on tables inside the store.

8. The storeowner (surprise / surprises) the people in the street.

9. She (open / opens) the doors of the store a day early to meet the crowds.

10. We (think / thinks) she will have a very successful store.

Talk About Yourself

First-person narratives are written from the point of view of the author. The word *I* is used to describe the writer. First-person narratives can be fiction or nonfiction.

Write a first-person narrative that describes something you did this week. Remember to use *I* and to write from your point of view.

_____

_____

_____

_____

_____

_____

_____

_____

_____

_____

_____

_____

_____

_____

_____

_____

_____

To the Root of It All

A **root word** is a smaller word that makes up a longer word. A prefix, suffix, or both word parts can be added to a root to make a new word with a related but new meaning.

For example:
The root word of <u>mistaken</u> is *mistake*.
The root word of <u>registration</u> is *register*.

Look at each word.
Write the root word on the line.

Look at each word.
Add a prefix or suffix to make a new word.

1. recondition _____

2. extraordinary _____

3. reconsider _____

4. unpopularity _____

5. scientist _____

6. alphabetical _____

7. medication _____

8. discuss _____

9. final _____

10. absolute _____

11. energy _____

12. fill _____

13. write _____

14. pharmacy _____

Let's Compare

A **comparative** adjective tells how something is more or less like something else.
A **superlative** adjective tells how something is most or least like other things. Comparatives often use the suffix –*er*. Superlatives often use the suffix –*est*.
Exceptions include good, better, and best.

For example:

Adjective	Comparative	Superlative
ugly	uglier	ugliest
round	rounder	roundest

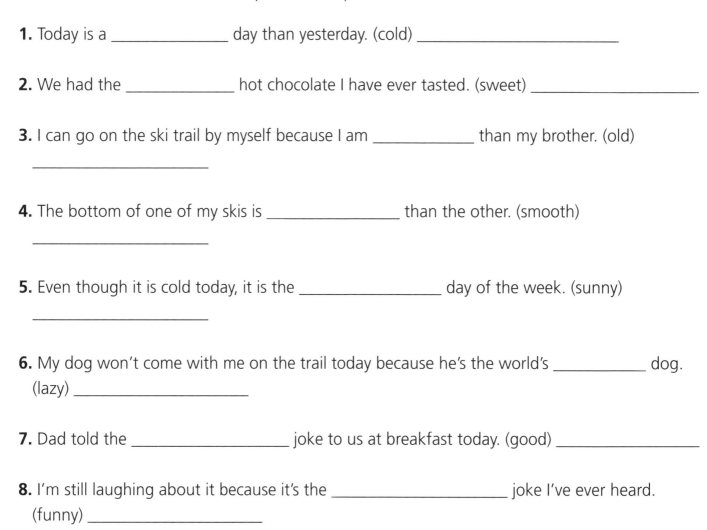

Complete each sentence. Write the correct form of the word in parentheses.
Then write whether
the word is *comparative* or *superlative*.

1. Today is a _____ day than yesterday. (cold) _____

2. We had the _____ hot chocolate I have ever tasted. (sweet) _____

3. I can go on the ski trail by myself because I am _____ than my brother. (old)
_____

4. The bottom of one of my skis is _____ than the other. (smooth)
_____

5. Even though it is cold today, it is the _____ day of the week. (sunny)
_____

6. My dog won't come with me on the trail today because he's the world's _____ dog.
(lazy) _____

7. Dad told the _____ joke to us at breakfast today. (good) _____

8. I'm still laughing about it because it's the _____ joke I've ever heard.
(funny) _____

There's the Proof!

Proofreading is reading what you have written to try to find errors. When you proofread, you may find many kinds of errors, but keep an eye out especially for errors in punctuation, spelling, and grammar.

Read the paragraph carefully. Rewrite it to fix any errors you see.

Jackson has always been obsess with tiger. Ever since he were a littel boy, he has been asking his parents for tiger print wallpaper for his room. He has six stuffed animal of tigers and 12 books about tigers and their habitats eating habits and adaptations He has been to the local zoo about once a month to visit the tigers their. He has come to no them all by name. Jackson's mom thinks that he should write to the zoo to asks for a special zoo tour.

_____

_____

_____

_____

_____

_____

_____

Read each sentence carefully to look for errors. Rewrite each sentence so that it is correct.

1. There is a new parks being builts on Rayborne avenue.

_____

2. My olders Brother is one of the construction workers on the sight.

_____

3. He say its going to be the best park around town because it have a hedge maize.

_____

Did I Persuade You?

Writing can **persuade**, or convince, the reader of something. Persuasive writing often uses opinions to make the reader believe or understand the author's point of view.

Read the passage and answer the questions below.

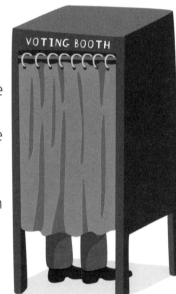

Dear Ms. Mayor,

I hope you can help me with my problem. I think there should be more people to help run the election centers in town this Election Day. Last year, I waited with my mom for an hour and a half to vote because there were problems with the voting machines and not enough people to help. As a result of this, I was late for school and my mom was late for work. I saw a lot of people walk away from the voting booths when they saw the lines because they did not have time to wait.

If there were just a few more people there last time, things would have run a lot more smoothly. If you can ask some more people to give their time to help out on Election Day, I think you'll see a great turnout and a successful voting day. I would love to help myself, but I am too young.

Thanks for listening to my problem. I think it has a very simple solution.

Sincerely,

Sanjay Patel

1. What is the problem that the author points out to the mayor?

_____

_____

2. What is the author trying to persuade the mayor to do?

_____

_____

3. Why does the author think his solution will work?

_____

_____

Making It Happen

A **cause** makes something happen. An **effect** is what happens as a result. There are many causes and effects in writing. Sometimes a cause has more than one effect. Sometimes an effect has more than one cause.

For example:
The child cried in the restaurant because it was out of macaroni and cheese.
Cause: The restaurant was out of macaroni and cheese.
Effect: The child cried.

Read each cause below. Then write an effect.

1. **Cause:** It was raining on Halloween night.
   Effect: _____

2. **Cause:** When Mom walked through the door, we jumped from behind the couch and yelled "Surprise!"
   Effect: _____

3. **Cause:** I didn't study for the science test.
   Effect: _____

4. **Cause:** Dad watered the lawn every night for two weeks.
   Effect: _____

5. **Cause:** Ben's glasses broke when he dropped them on the floor.
   Effect: _____

6. **Cause:** Sara and Louis stopped eating sweets and started exercising every day.
   Effect: _____

Running On and On and On

A **run-on sentence** is an incorrect sentence that joins two independent clauses without using punctuation or conjunctions. To avoid run-on sentences, use a comma or conjunction to join the two clauses, or turn a run-on sentence into two sentences.

For example:
Run-on: The bicycle race starts at 11:30 we might not make it on time.
Correct: The bicycle race starts at 11:30. We might not make it on time.

Rewrite each run-on sentence twice. First, make it one compound sentence. Next, make it into two simple sentences.

1. Dad raced us toward the parking lot we were five minutes late.

   _____
   _____

2. After dropping us off, he went to the parent area we took our bikes to the starting line.

   _____
   _____

3. The race official quickly handed us our numbers Sara needed help to put hers on.

   _____
   _____

4. I was nervous to see all of the other bikers standing at the starting line it would be a few more minutes until I was ready.

   _____
   _____

5. "One minute until the starting gun goes off," said the official my heart began racing even faster.

   _____
   _____

Find the Conjunction

A **conjunction** joins words or phrases together. The words *and, but, yet, so,* and *or* are conjunctions.

For example:
I don't like grape gum, <u>but</u> I love the taste of grapes.
You don't know much about the Civil War, <u>so</u> let's get studying.
Take me with you to the movies, <u>or</u> drop me off at home.

Combine the phrases into one sentence using a conjunction. Use correct capitalization and punctuation in your sentence.

1. You're up so late tonight   it's time to get some sleep

_____

2. I know that is a really good book   you have to put it down now

_____

3. I'm going to turn off the light now   don't get startled

_____

4. We can go to the beach tomorrow   you can bring the book with you

_____

Read each sentence. Circle the conjunction. Underline the words or phrases it joins.

5. During the American Revolution, colonists became free from England and we drafted our own constitution.

6. George Washington led the colonial army, but Thomas Jefferson had the role of writing the Declaration of Independence.

7. In the Civil War, the northern and southern states fought each other, and some families were divided as a result.

8. States from the South were called the Confederacy, and states from the North were called the Union.

Here's My Plan

A good writer plans out what he or she will write before beginning. A **graphic organizer** can help you record your thoughts and organize your ideas.

Think of a topic for a fiction story. Write the main idea in the center oval of the concept map below. Then put details in the surrounding ovals. Write your story on a separate sheet of paper.

Causes and Effects

Remember: A **cause** is a reason something happens. An **effect** is something that happens as a result of something else. You can notice some cause-and-effect patterns when you read. Words such as *because of* and *as a result* are clues to look for a cause-and-effect relationship.

Read the passage and answer the questions below.

Ashley loved Blueberry Dream cereal more than anything. As soon as she woke up every morning, she went to the kitchen and poured a huge bowl to enjoy. One morning, her mom went to the cabinet for her own breakfast. "Maybe I'll have some Blueberry Dream," she said.

Ashley's mom was shocked to find the Blueberry Dream almost gone. "What's happening here?" she asked. "I bought this cereal only a couple days ago!"

"It's the best cereal, Mom," said Ashley. "I eat it because it's so good. Next time we need to buy more of it so it lasts longer. It's a healthy cereal, right?"

"Well," said her mom. "I guess it's OK to eat a lot of it because it is healthy. I'll get more from the store today." But what should I eat right now? she wondered.

1. What caused the Blueberry Dream cereal to disappear so quickly?

_____

_____

_____

2. What effect did talking to her mom have for Ashley?

_____

_____

_____

3. What caused Ashley's mom to agree with Ashley?

_____

_____

_____

May I Ask You a Few Questions?

One kind of writing is called **reporting**. Newspaper reporters often interview their subjects to get important information from them for a story. An interview is a session of questions and answers about a topic.

Write interview questions for a person you know so that you can learn something about him or her. Then ask the person the questions and record the answers.

1. Question:

_____

_____

_____

_____

Answer:

_____

_____

_____

_____

2. Question:

_____

_____

_____

_____

Answer:

_____

_____

_____

_____

3. Question:

_____

_____

_____

_____

Answer:

_____

_____

_____

_____

4. Question:

_____

_____

_____

_____

Answer:

_____

_____

_____

_____

Writing from an Interview

After a writer has conducted an **interview** with someone, the interview can be written as an article or other expository writing. The answers to the interview questions become the information in the piece of writing.

Use the interview below with principal Bill Ching to write a short article about him.

Question: What was the first thing you wanted to do as principal of the school?

Answer: When I first got here, I noticed that the buses arrived at the school late almost every day. So I changed the bus schedules and routes so that students were on time for their busy school day.

Question: What would you like to change about the school in the future?

Answer: I would like to have more parents help with small projects at the school. We need parent volunteers to give kids extra help in reading and math.

_____

_____

_____

_____

_____

_____

_____

_____

_____

_____

_____

_____

_____

_____

Make a Note of It!

Good writers take **notes** about their topic before they begin to write. Recording your main ideas and supporting details will help you stay organized and focus on what you will be writing about.

Use books, encyclopedias, or the Internet to research an animal of your choice. Write five facts about the animal. Then use the facts to write a paragraph sharing what you've learned.

Animal: _____

1. _____

2. _____

3. _____

4. _____

5. _____

_____

_____

_____

_____

_____

_____

_____

_____

_____

_____

_____

_____

Let's Be Less Wordy

When writing, we sometimes use more words than needed. Think about ways to say the same thing in a clearer way by using **fewer words**.

For example:
Wordy: Let's go to a store where groceries are sold and buy some fruit that is round and red and grows on trees!
Improvement: Let's go to the grocery store to buy some apples.

Rewrite each sentence so that the underlined section is less wordy.

1. The <u>person who works behind the counter collecting people's money</u> said that the bananas are on sale this week.

_____

2. When I choose the fruit, I make sure they are <u>not too old, but old enough to taste the way they should</u>.

_____

3. Sometimes, there is a long <u>gathering of people waiting to check out</u> at the front counter.

_____

4. I checked my <u>written record of things that I would need at the grocery store</u> to see if I forgot anything.

_____

5. I put everything into the <u>wheeled carriage that holds grocery items</u> and walked up and down the aisles.

_____

6. It would be great to have <u>some foods to keep me from getting hungry before dinner</u>.

_____

Where's the Sentence?

A **sentence** is a group of words that expresses a complete idea or thought. A sentence starts with a capital letter and ends with a period, exclamation point, or question mark. A sentence must have a subject and a verb to be complete.

For example:
Incomplete: friends baked a pie.
Complete: Julia was happy because her friends baked a pie.

Circle *complete* or *incomplete* for each sentence below.
Rewrite incomplete sentences to make complete sentences
with correct punctuation and capitalization.

1. Polar bears and their habitats are being threatened.
   complete   incomplete

_____

2. many species of polar bears.
   complete   incomplete

_____

3. There are close to 25,000 polar bears on earth.
   complete   incomplete

_____

4. Polar bears are adapted to extremely cold conditions.
   complete   incomplete

_____

5. These beautiful animals live in the Arctic.
   complete   incomplete

_____

6. live among icy habitats in ocean environments.
   complete   incomplete

_____

Order, Everyone!

Remember, **sequence** is the order in which events happen. When reading, pay attention to the sequence of events. This will help you to understand the story better.

Number the events below in the correct order.

_____ Miguel's mom handed the money to the cashier and Miguel smiled widely. He couldn't wait to get it home and play it. This was going to be a great birthday.

_____ "Miguel," yelled Mom from the kitchen. "Try some of this hot chocolate while you are waiting. It might cheer you up." The drink was Miguel's favorite. He was feeling better already.

_____ As he reached for the power button of his video game system, he noticed that the red light was out. "What!" he cried.

_____ Miguel loved to play video games. He stood in front of the video game shelves in the store and wondered what to buy.

_____ "I forgot to tell you," called Dad from the other room. "We had a power outage earlier and some of the circuits are still not working correctly. You'll have to keep the system off for a couple more hours."

_____ Miguel couldn't believe his ears. He couldn't play his new game for hours! Why did this have to happen to him?

Compound Word Hunt

A **compound word** is made of two smaller words. The meaning of the compound word can usually be found by looking at the meaning of the words that make it up.

Use each compound word in a sentence.

1. backhand _____

2. brainwash _____

3. copywriter _____

4. crybaby _____

5. drawbridge _____

6. freethinker _____

7. handcuff _____

8. homeward _____

9. landslide _____

10. meantime _____

11. outburst _____

12. overcapacity _____

13. overreact _____

14. praiseworthy _____

15. sidetrack _____

16. underbelly _____

A Story in the Middle of It All

A good story has a beginning, a middle, and an end. In the **middle** of the story, the focus is on the problem, or conflict. We have already been introduced to the characters and are becoming more involved with what they are doing.

Read the beginning and end of the story below.
Write a middle part for the story.

Meg walked the same path to school every day. For the past two days, though, an adorable Labrador retriever puppy followed her and then wandered happily into Cunningham Park. Today when Meg got to the edge of the park, she saw a sign on a telephone pole. "Lost Dog," it said. "Goes by the name Tootsie. If found, please call 555-2993." And there, staring back at Meg, was a picture of her new puppy friend.

_____

_____

_____

_____

_____

_____

_____

_____

_____

_____

_____

_____

_____

_____

_____

As Meg rang the doorbell, Tootsie was already wagging her tail, whining, and scratching happily at the door. "Just a minute," Meg said, pulling on her collar to keep her close by. "You'll be home in a minute!"

Fun with Compound Predicates

> A **compound predicate** is more than one predicate with the same subject. The words *and* and *or* are often used to connect predicates in a sentence.
>
> For example:
> I do homework during the week <u>and</u> play soccer on the weekends.
> My brother will help to do my homework <u>or</u> kick a ball around.

Read each sentence. Underline each predicate.
Circle the word that joins them to make a compound predicate.

1. We laugh at his jokes and listen to the tape again.

2. Josh wants to be a comedian and writes his own jokes.

3. His mom takes him to auditions and waits for him in the car.

4. She hears laughter coming from inside the auditorium, and smiles.

5. Josh's mom sticks with her kids and helps them when they need it.

6. Josh came out of the auditorium smiling and walked to the car.

7. He felt like he had just won a million bucks and acted like it, too.

8. His mom called out from the car and cheered for him.

9. Josh thanked all of his friends for helping him, but thanked his mom first.

Quoting Correctly

Quotation marks tell the reader when dialogue begins and ends. The first word in a quotation is capitalized. A comma is used at the end of a quotation that does not appear at the end of a sentence. Each time new dialogue begins, a new paragraph starts.

For example:
"Marcus is the best singer in this rock band," said Julio.

Rewrite the paragraph below so that the quotation marks, punctuation, and capitalization are used correctly.

I love to sing I told Julio. But I don't think I can sing in front of an audience. Julio answered just pretend the audience is not there. Don't think about them and you can concentrate on singing. I told Julio what I thought. I have tried all sorts of tricks, I told him. Nothing works. I would much rather just play my guitar and not worry about singing. Alright he said. But if you change your mind, there is an opening in our band for a rock star!

_____

_____

_____

_____

_____

_____

_____

_____

_____

_____

_____

Catch Those Good Ideas on Paper!

A good writer will **brainstorm** a list of ideas and concepts that would make good writing topics. After reviewing the list, a writer can choose the best topic.

For example:
For a science biography project, here's a possible list of topics: Marie Curie, Thomas Edison, Aristotle, Albert Einstein, Isaac Newton, Charles Darwin, Jane Goodall, Rachel Carson, Alexander Graham Bell, Edward Jenner

Brainstorm a list of topics for a report about severe weather and storms. Then choose one of the topics from the list. Research and write a paragraph about the topic on the right side of the page.

_____   _____
_____   _____
_____   _____
_____   _____
_____   _____
_____   _____
_____   _____
_____   _____
_____   _____
_____   _____
_____   _____
_____   _____
_____   _____
_____   _____
_____   _____

Albert Einstein
Isaac Newton
Jane Goodall

I Like Your Viewpoint

An author's **viewpoint** is the way an author feels about a subject or idea. An author can express a viewpoint in nonfiction works, such as in magazine or newspaper articles.

For example:
Viewpoint 1: The best way for children to learn their multiplication facts is to memorize them.
Viewpoint 2: The best way for children to learn their multiplication facts is to use a number line.

Read the passage and answer the questions below.

What's the best way to teach students how to multiply? They must be taught the concept of multiplication as repeated addition, or they will never truly understand multiplication at all. Many teachers just make students memorize the multiplication table so that they can do problem after problem quickly. This method does not benefit students and they are not really learning at all.

MULTIPLICATION TABLE

	1	2	3	4	5	6	7	8	9
1	1	2	3	4	5	6	7	8	9
2	2	4	6	8	10	12	14	16	18
3	3	6	9	12	15	18	21	24	27
4	4	8	12	16	20	24	28	32	36
5	5	10	15	20	25	30	35	40	45
6	6	12	18	24	30	36	42	48	54
7	7	14	21	28	35	42	49	56	63
8	8	16	24	32	40	48	56	64	72
9	9	18	27	36	45	54	63	72	81

Instead of just memorizing that $7 \times 7 = 49$, students have to understand that 7×7 is the same as saying $7 + 7$ again and again until they have done it seven times. With that knowledge, students can solve any multiplication problem they want to. However, when they only know how to memorize, they are not learning the concepts behind the math. This will make it difficult for them to be able to solve real-life problems.

1. What is the author's viewpoint about learning multiplication?

   _____

   _____

2. What is the author's viewpoint about memorizing the multiplication table?

   _____

   _____

3. What is your viewpoint about the subject?

   _____

   _____

Who Does This Belong To?

A **possessive** noun shows who owns something. When using the possessive of a singular noun, add an apostrophe and *s* in most cases. When using the possessive of a plural noun ending in *s*, add an apostrophe after the *s*. If the plural noun does not end in *s*, add an apostrophe and *s*.

For example:
Singular: Sue's notebook   a friend's joke
Plural: the classes' performance   the children's books

Look at each word. Write the singular possessive form.

1. secretary _____

2. farmer _____

3. physicist _____

4. airport _____

5. eggplant _____

6. family _____

7. essay _____

8. uncle _____

9. president _____

10. Larry _____

Look at each word. Write the plural possessive form.

11. onions _____

12. mice _____

13. candies _____

14. coats _____

15. parachutes _____

16. people _____

17. balloons _____

18. sweaters _____

19. janitors _____

20. companies _____

Rewrite each phrase using possessive nouns.

21. the treat of the dog _____

22. the wheels of the car _____

23. the pages of the book _____

24. the efforts of the students _____

25. the parking spaces of the stores _____

What a Comparison!

A **comparative** adjective compares two or more things. Words like *more* and *less* can help make a comparison. An *–er* ending on an adjective also makes a word comparative.

A **superlative** adjective compares more than two things. The word ending *–est* makes a superlative. You can also add the words *least* or *most* before the adjective to make it superlative.

For example:

Comparative: funnier   more confused
Superlative: funniest   most confused

Read each item. Check whether it is *comparative* or *superlative*.

	comparative	superlative
1. less disgusting		
2. likeliest		
3. more experienced		
4. thinner		
5. more exaggerated		
6. smartest		
7. most inspired		
8. dirtier		
9. least understood		
10. less annoyed		
11. more prepared		
12. foggiest		

Rewrite each sentence so that the comparative adjective becomes superlative.

13. Jessica's class is quieter than Ashley's.

_____

14. It is less expensive to fill up Ravi's car with gas than it is to fill up Cori's car.

_____

15. The first play was more entertaining than the second one.

_____

Adverbs Everywhere

An **adverb** describes a verb or an adjective. An adverb can even describe another adverb. Many adverbs end in –*ly*. They answer questions about the word they modify, such as *when, how, where*, or *to what extent*.

For example:
The dog's tail wagged *happily*.
The pet store closed *late*.
A puppy sale was being discussed *carefully* by the family.

Read each sentence. Underline the adverb. Then write your own sentence that uses the adverb.

1. The puppy looked cautiously through the door of his new home.

_____

2. He wanted to stay outside.

_____

3. But Noah pushed the dog playfully from behind.

_____

4. Noah had waited patiently for a dog since he was two years old.

_____

5. The dog inspected the house nervously.

_____

6. The dog would be very happy here.

_____

7. Then he barked loudly at the cat.

_____

8. Maybe he would not adjust quickly.

_____

You're a Character!

A **character** is a person or animal in a story. The way a character looks, acts, and feels are all part of the story. Details about a character help to make the story more interesting.

For example:
The story "Hansel and Gretel" includes a character who lives in a gingerbread house. Her character can be described as a mean old woman.

Think of a character you know from a story. Write a description of the character. Include as many details as possible to describe the character.

_____

_____

_____

_____

_____

_____

_____

_____

_____

_____

_____

_____

_____

_____

_____

_____

_____

_____

Fact or Opinion?

Any kind of writing can have facts and opinions, whether the writing is fiction or nonfiction. A **fact** is a statement that can be proven. An **opinion** is the way someone thinks or feels. An opinion cannot be proven.

For example:
Fact: Cell phones are more portable than phones on a regular landline.
Opinion: Cell phone quality is not as good as the quality of landlines.

Read the passage and complete the chart with facts and opinions.

The telephone was invented in 1876 by Alexander Graham Bell. Since that time, there have been many improvements to the telephone. During the late 1800s and early 1900s, networks of telephone lines expanded throughout the country and throughout the world. People loved the new technology. They used it to keep in touch with loved ones and do business. The phone became an important part of our lives.

Then, in the 1940s, the technology for cellular phones was invented. It did not become popular or commercialized until the 1980s, after it went through many improvements. The first cell phones were large and cumbersome. People who use cell phones today would not enjoy using one of the first cell phones. They were difficult to use and did not sound good. The cell phones we use today are revolutionary. They have changed our lives for the better.

Facts	Opinions

Holy Homograph!

Homographs are words that have the same spelling but different meanings. Some homographs have different pronunciations.

For example:
Wally did not feel *well* after drinking from the *well*.

Read each sentence. Write a new sentence using another meaning for the underlined homograph.

1. Alec's teacher thought a lack of attention was the <u>root</u> of his problem.

_____

2. Some materials expand and <u>contract</u> with changing temperatures.

_____

3. Amy was proud of her <u>Polish</u> ancestry.

_____

4. The safety commissioner will check for any toxic <u>refuse</u> left at the landfill.

_____

5. Jamie would never <u>desert</u> her teammates the morning of a swim meet.

_____

6. Lori made a graph with the x and y <u>axes</u> intersecting.

_____

7. The speaker will <u>address</u> the crowd in 45 minutes.

_____

8. Jenna sat in the back <u>row</u> with her aunt and uncle.

_____

A Picture Tells a Story

Descriptive writing uses details to tell about something. Describing what you see in a picture is one way to practice writing detailed information.

For example:
If you see a picture of a boy getting off a school bus, you can write about *who* the boy is, *where* he is coming from, and *where* he is going. You can describe the bus and what it looks like and give information about the boy.

Look at the picture below. Describe what you see. Make up details about the characters and events. Write a short story with as many details as you can.

_____

_____

_____

_____

_____

_____

_____

_____

_____

_____

_____

Connotations

A **connotation** is the way the meaning of a word sounds to the reader. A connotation can be positive or negative.

For example:
Positive connotation: The game system in our house is a <u>classic</u>.
Negative connotation: The game system in our house is <u>old</u>.

Complete each sentence. Circle the word in parentheses that has a more positive connotation in the context of the sentence.

1. In order to protect his friends, Miguel was being (sneaky / secretive) about the journey.

2. They packed the car with (junk / supplies) that they would need.

3. They stopped to fill the gas tank and then (continued / sped) along their way.

4. I (doubt / wonder) if they will be back soon.

5. I can hear their dog (barking / yapping) in the background.

Complete each sentence. Circle the word in parentheses that has a more negative connotation in the context of the sentence.

6. Janie is (eager / impatient) about beginning work at the magazine.

7. She thinks she will enjoy being a (mean / firm) boss to the other employees.

8. Most people think the magazine is too (serious / boring).

9. Janie would like to (change / destroy) the magazine's image.

10. Millions of subscribers could be (surprised / angered) by her decisions.

Creating Prepositional Phrases

A **preposition** is a word that shows the relation between a noun or pronoun and the rest of the sentence. Prepositions can tell about position or time, such as *in, on, below, at, without, after,* and *before*. A **prepositional phrase** is made up of a preposition and the phrase that it describes.

For example:
We will have dinner *after the show*.
after is the preposition. The prepositional phrase is *after the show*.

Read each sentence. Circle the preposition. Underline the prepositional phrase. Then write your own sentence using the prepositional phrase.

1. Fox chased Cat into the woods.

_____

2. This was a crafty thing to do, because Cat immediately felt lost in the strange environment.

_____

3. Foxes are crafty creatures, or so it says in the history books.

_____

4. While Cat was lost, Fox ran to Cat's house.

_____

Read each sentence and find more than one prepositional phrase in each. Underline each one.

5. Fox stuffed his pockets with goodies from Cat's refrigerator.

6. Then Fox returned to the woods with a smile on his face.

7. "If you're lost, you can come with me," said Fox. "I'll be nice to you."

8. Cat followed Fox near the stream and they both sat there quietly on a log.

Compare It and Contrast It

Before you write, it helps to **organize** your thoughts and think about what you want to say. When you write about two things that can be compared or contrasted, a Venn diagram is a good way to keep track of ideas. Remember that to compare means to tell how things are alike, while contrast means to tell how things are different.

Choose two of your favorite childhood toys to compare. How were they alike and different? Use the Venn diagram to keep track of your ideas.

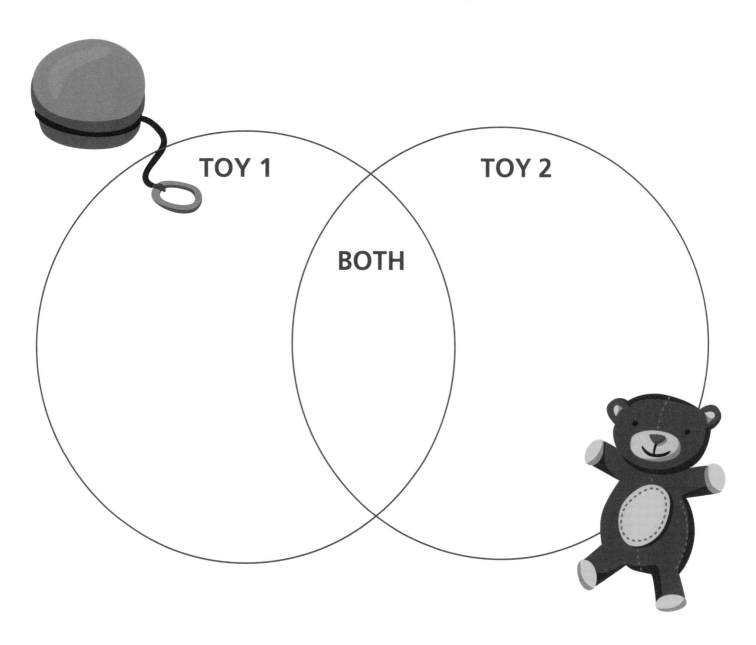

TOY 1

TOY 2

BOTH

Tell Me How To

How-to writing describes how to do things. It uses descriptive writing and tells the steps of a process in order. Recipes, directions, and owner's manuals are examples of how-to writing.

Think of something you know how to do well.
Write directions for someone to explain how to do it.

_____

_____

_____

_____

_____

_____

_____

_____

_____

_____

_____

_____

_____

_____

_____

_____

What Do You Learn from That?

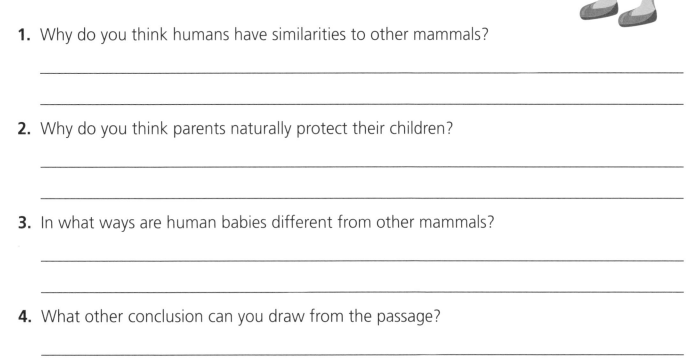

When you **draw conclusions**, you use what you know and what you have read to make decisions about something.

For example:
Students who learn how to play and read musical notes have a better understanding of math concepts such as fractions.
Conclusion: Musical notes represent fractions.

Read the passage and answer the questions below by drawing conclusions.

Human babies are not the only mammals that learn by trial and error. Many mammals show some of the same learning behaviors that humans show. As babies, many mammals rely heavily on their parents for help catching their own food, keeping up with the pack, or staying out of danger. After a while, they are ready to venture out on their own. However, gaining total independence takes time. A mother bear will stay close by her cub until she feels that it can handle dangers on its own. Much like a human baby, a bear cub is protected until it is ready to face the world.

1. Why do you think humans have similarities to other mammals?

_____

_____

2. Why do you think parents naturally protect their children?

_____

_____

3. In what ways are human babies different from other mammals?

_____

_____

4. What other conclusion can you draw from the passage?

_____

_____

You're a Poet!

A **poem** is a piece of writing that expresses feelings or describes images in an interesting way. Rhythmic phrases are used instead of sentences. Some poems rhyme in a repeating pattern, but many do not.

Think about a poem topic that you would like to write about. Use the space below to record your ideas. Then write your poem.

Topic: _____

Rhyming or not rhyming? _____

If rhyming, what is the pattern? _____

Details

_____

_____

_____

Images to describe

_____

_____

_____

Poem _____

_____

_____

_____

_____

_____

_____

_____

Is That a Fact?

When you read, you will come across some statements that are fact and some that are opinion. Remember: A **fact** can be proven. An **opinion** cannot be proven.

Read the passage. Then write *fact* or *opinion* for the sentences below.

Max is running for class president to try to get us new cafeteria tables. He said he would try to raise money by having car washes, bake sales, and other events around the school. Carrie is running for class president so that she can get students more decision-making power in the school. She said she would try to meet with the principal every week to ask her about new issues that affect the students.

I would much rather have new cafeteria tables than to have to make decisions with the principal. The cafeteria tables are about 20 years old. Some of them look like they are about to fall over. I wish everyone would vote for Max.

1. He said he would try to raise money by having car washes, bake sales, and other events around the school. _____

2. Carrie is running for class president so that she can get students more decision-making power in the school. _____

3. I would much rather have new cafeteria tables than to have to make decisions with the principal. _____

4. The cafeteria tables are about 20 years old. _____

5. Some of them look like they are about to fall over. _____

6. I wish everyone would vote for Max. _____

Writing in the Right Order

It makes sense to write information about an event or a process in **order**. Tell about what happened *first, next*, and *last*. This will make your writing more organized and easier to understand.

Use the chart below to tell about something that happened to you today. Then write about it in an interesting way.

FIRST	NEXT	LAST

_____

_____

_____

_____

_____

_____

_____

_____

What Happened Next?

Most fiction stories have a beginning, a middle, and an end. A story ending is a **conclusion** that resolves the problem, or conflict, that has been happening in the story.

Read the story below. Write a conclusion that will resolve the problem, or conflict.

Lanie has wanted to be a superhero ever since she was a toddler. When she found out that people couldn't really fly, she cried in her bedroom for an hour. Then she decided that if she couldn't be a real superhero, she would be an everyday hero who tried to help other people. She volunteered at hospitals, soup kitchens, and schools. She helped as many people in need as she could. Her problem was that she still didn't feel like a superhero.

_____

_____

_____

_____

_____

_____

_____

_____

_____

_____

_____

_____

_____

You've Convinced Me!

A **persuasive letter** explains the writer's viewpoint about something and tries to get the reader to agree. Like any letter, a persuasive letter has an opening and closing.

Imagine that your town has just passed a law that prevents children from visiting the new art museum. What do you think of this law? Write a letter to your town mayor to explain your point of view.

_____

_____

_____

_____

_____

_____

_____

_____

_____

_____

_____

_____

_____

_____

_____

_____

_____

_____

What Are We Describing?

Remember: An **adverb** is a word that describes a verb, adjective, or other adverb. Adverbs often end in –ly. An **adjective** is a word that describes a noun.

For example:
Adverb: The kitten <u>purred</u> *softly*.   (*Softly* describes the verb <u>purred</u>.)
Adjective: That is a *loud* <u>dog</u>.   (*Loud* describes the noun <u>dog</u>.)

Complete each sentence with the correct word in parentheses. Underline what is being described.

1. Sabrina played the flute (beautiful / beautifully) in the concert last night.

2. She practiced long, (hard / hardly) hours this past week to get her solo right.

3. The audience was so (quiet / quietly) when she began to play.

4. Then I heard people cheer (wild / wildly) when she was finished.

5. Her music teacher watched the audience and then gave Sabrina an (approving / approvingly) glance from backstage.

6. At first, Sabrina was (nervous / nervously) to go onstage in front of everyone.

7. Now that she knows that she can perform (handsome / handsomely) in front of crowds, she'll do another solo again next year.

8. She smiled (polite / politely) at the crowd and took a bow.

9. Sabrina's parents walked a (stunning / stunningly) bouquet of flowers to the stage for her to accept.

Tell Me All About It

Plot describes the events of a story, including the story's problem, or conflict. When you describe what a story is about, you are describing its plot.

For example:
In the plot of *The Polar Express*, a young boy goes on a magical journey to help him decide whether he still believes in Santa Claus.

Choose one of your favorite stories. Explain the plot of the story.

Explain It to Me

Expository writing is meant to explain, inform, define, or instruct. Expository writing uses supporting details, descriptive language, and a logical order. Most expository writing is nonfiction.

For example:
Hurricanes can sometimes be identified incorrectly as tsunamis in the Pacific Ocean. Because the storm surges these hurricanes create can be so large and cover such a big area, they resemble tsunamis.

Research a nonfiction topic. Write an expository paragraph about the topic.

_____
_____
_____
_____
_____
_____
_____
_____
_____
_____
_____
_____
_____
_____

Thinking About Time and Place

Setting is the time and place in which a story takes place. A story can take place anywhere and at any time, including in the past, present, or future. The setting can be important to the plot of the story, or it can be secondary to the story.

For example:
Setting: A zoo in the future
Tito wanted to see the giraffes, so he entered the Quick Pod labeled "Giraffes" and pushed the button. He was suddenly transported into the section of the zoo where the giraffes were held.

Write a story that takes place in a different time and place than where you are today. Make sure you describe the setting in detail.

_____

_____

_____

_____

_____

_____

_____

_____

_____

_____

_____

_____

_____

If at First You Don't Succeed...

Remember: A **revision** is a writing stage in which errors are fixed and improvements are made to a draft. Revisions often address errors in spelling, punctuation, and grammar. They also reword sentences to improve how they sound.

Read the draft below. Write a revision in the space provided.
Fix errors and try to make the text read better.

Namita bit into the granola bare and started chewing. Ow, she thought to hersel. Why does that tooth bother me every time I eat? she asked herself. She hated going to the dentist but she was lucky enough to never have had a cavity. Now she wondered if her luck had been run out and if this is what a cavity feel like. She put the granola bar down and went to talks to her mom. "I need to see the dentist she said sadly.

_____
_____
_____
_____
_____
_____
_____
_____
_____
_____
_____

Make a Comparison

Comparative writing tells how things are alike and different. Remember, when you compare, you tell how things are alike. When you contrast, you tell how things are different.

Use the Venn diagram below to compare and contrast your favorite and least favorite season.

This Is My Story

Narrative writing tells a story. It usually has a plot, a beginning, a middle, an end, and a conflict that must be resolved. A narrative pays special attention to the main character's point of view.

Imagine that you just won a million dollars.
Write a narrative to tell how you feel and what you are experiencing.

_____

_____

_____

_____

_____

_____

_____

_____

_____

_____

_____

_____

_____

_____

_____

_____

Pronouns for You and Me

A **possessive pronoun** shows who owns something. The most common possessive pronouns are *my, your, our, their, his, her,* and *its.* Use *mine, yours, ours, theirs, his,* and *hers* when replacing nouns.

Complete each sentence by circling the correct pronoun in parentheses.

1. The restaurant was crowded with _____ friends. (our / mine)

2. We can always pull up a seat to sit with _____. (they / them)

3. The chef said he would make a specialty dessert for _____. (us / my)

4. My friends were very kind to come out and support _____ tonight. (me / my)

5. There's nothing like good friends and _____ smiling faces. (them / their)

Rewrite each sentence. Replace the underlined part using a possessive pronoun.

6. The train picked up the eager passengers and <u>the</u> heavy luggage <u>that belongs to them</u>.

_____

7. The last stop on the train route is <u>the one that belongs to Jake and Ravi</u>.

_____

8. One of the first stops on the train is <u>the one that belongs to me</u>.

_____

9. Which stop is <u>the one that belongs to you</u>?

_____

Where Do the Commas Go?

A **comma** is often used before the words *and, or*, and *but* and after words like *first, next,* and *last*. Commas also separate compound sentences and separate words in a list.

For example:
Mix the flour, sugar, baking soda, and salt in a large bowl.
Next, add two eggs and stir the mixture until everything is blended.

Add commas to each sentence to make it correct.

1. The community center offers field trips picnics movie nights and holiday gatherings.

2. Next week Theresa Paco Jorge and Jay are organizing an event in honor of Veterans Day.

3. They may not have enough volunteers but they will continue with their planning anyway.

4. They are asking guests to bring various cakes cookies brownies and other baked goods.

5. People should know however that there will be no refrigerator available for people to store food.

6. First they will hang posters in the community center to advertise the event.

7. Then they will hang similar posters in the park local schools and along Main Street.

8. They wanted to put an advertisement in the newspaper but they did not have a budget for it.

9. Events at the community center always have a good turnout so they are pretty sure that there will be a lot of people to enjoy the event with them.

10. My mom dad grandmother and uncle will be at the event; however they heard there will be rain that day.

Plural Possessives

A **plural possessive noun** shows the ownership of something by more than one person or thing. For nouns that do not end in *s*, add an apostrophe and *s*. For nouns that end in *s*, just add an apostrophe.

For example:
I have seen the *routes of the buses*.   I have seen the <u>buses' routes</u>.
We see the *homes of the families*.   We can see the <u>families' homes</u>.

Rewrite each sentence without plural possessive nouns.

1. April commented on the <u>books' plots</u>.

_____

2. The series is my <u>friends' favorites</u>.

_____

3. We like to see them on <u>libraries' shelves</u>.

_____

Rewrite each sentence. Make a plural possessive noun out of the underlined part.

4. The family reunion was the <u>idea of the cousins</u>.

_____

5. They sent out the <u>invitations of the uncles</u>.

_____

6. We asked for the <u>recipes of the families</u>.

_____

7. Some people were unhappy with the <u>volume of the songs</u>.

_____

Which Word Should I Use?

Sometimes two words sound similar or have similar meanings and are easily confused with each other. Here are some common words that are often **misused** and confused with each other.

Complete each sentence. Circle the correct word in parentheses. Use a dictionary if you are unsure of which word is correct.

1. We split the food _____ the three boys. (among / between)

2. The _____ today looks like it will be beautiful. (weather / whether)

3. Jenny's shoes _____ her dress perfectly. (complement / compliment)

4. Our class understood everything _____ the last math section. (accept / except)

5. Dad always offers the best _____ he can. (advice / advise)

6. I never thought it was a good idea to _____ your money to Dave. (borrow / lend)

7. We will _____ five minutes to each section of the quiz. (a lot / allot)

8. When the girls stand _____ each other, I see that they look alike. (beside / besides)

9. We will put our differences _____ and get the job done. (aside / side)

10. The movie we saw last night was filled with special _____. (affects / effects)

Look at the Context, Get a Clue

A **context clue** is a hint that helps the reader figure out the meaning of an unknown word. Context clues can give a definition or an example of the unknown word. The clues are sometimes set off by commas.

For example:
Definition: We will <u>befriend</u>, or *make friends with*, the new kid at school.
Example: He was <u>arrogant</u>. He *thought he was the most important person there*.

Read each sentence. Write the meaning of the underlined word on the line. The context clues help define or illustrate the underlined word.

1. Lily thinks I should be more <u>assertive</u>, or bold.

_____

2. I will have to <u>recruit</u> more players to the team. I must convince them to join.

_____

3. Our practices have become like a <u>routine</u>, or habit.

_____

4. The road to the championship is <u>treacherous</u>. There are all sorts of hidden difficulties.

_____

5. The vote to buy new uniforms was <u>unanimous</u>. Everyone agreed.

_____

6. The ribbon <u>signifies</u>, or is a symbol of, your hard work.

_____

7. The 50-meter race is <u>strenuous</u> for most athletes. They have trouble doing it.

_____

8. A drink of water should <u>replenish</u> your energy, or make it return.

_____

Build a Word

Some words are made up of a combination of **prefixes**, **roots**, and **suffixes**.

Choose a word part from each box to make the words defined below.

prefix	root word	suffix
un- mis- re- pre-	introduce view necessary communicate	-tion -ly -ion -ing

1. act of introducing again

_____

2. act of not communicating properly

_____

3. in a manner that is not necessary

_____

4. process of viewing something again

_____

Look at each word. Write the meaning of the underlined word part.

5. scient<u>ist</u> _____

6. invent<u>or</u> _____

7. <u>re</u>living _____

8. <u>co</u>conspirator _____

9. <u>ex</u>pression _____

10. recharge<u>able</u> _____

Go Figure!

Figurative language can help make writing interesting. A **simile** is a figure of speech that uses the words *like* or *as* to compare things. A **metaphor** is a figure of speech that compares things *without* using *like* or *as*. **Alliteration** uses repeated consonant sounds in words, especially at the beginnings of words. **Onomatopoeia** uses words that mimic sounds.

For example:
Simile: The baby was as cute as a button.
Metaphor: The boy was boiling mad.
Alliteration: Sue's silly sister sat on the steps and sang.
Onomatopoeia: The buzz of the power saw is loud.

Read each sentence. What kind of figurative language is being used?
Write *simile, metaphor, alliteration,* or *onomatopoeia.*

1. George was as angry as a bull when he heard the news. _____

2. Cara's cooking could be considered creative yet comforting. _____

3. Davis made a pig of himself at the restaurant last night. _____

4. The *tick, tick, tick* of the clock made Jenny nervous that she would be late.

_____

5. Whatever Wanda wants, Wanda gets. _____

6. The weather report said it's raining cats and dogs! _____

7. We showered the man with compliments. _____

8. The *drip, drip* of the rain on the windowsill made Luis sleepy. _____

9. Rachel's directions were as clear as a bell. _____

10. Miguel's most memorable moment was masquerading as a madman.

_____

What's the Big Idea?

When reading a story, think about the **main idea** and **supporting details**. Remember, the main idea tells what the passage is mostly about. The supporting details help tell about the main idea.

Read the story. Then write the main idea and list the supporting details.

Colin was so excited when he was asked to test a new video game for a local company. His parents knew people who worked at the company, and they designed and created some of Colin's favorite video games. Colin felt like he couldn't wait for Thursday to come.

Once school was over on Thursday, his mom picked him up and drove him to the company. After his mom filled out some papers, they were brought to a big room to meet with a game designer named Robyn.

Robyn asked Colin many questions about each game and she carefully watched him play them. He told her what he liked and did not like about each game and what seemed too easy or too difficult for him. She told Colin that if he and his mom wanted, they could come back again next week. Colin's eyes lit up. He would come back anytime!

Main idea

_____

_____

_____

_____

Supporting details

_____

_____

_____

_____

Who's Confused?

People often get confused when using the words *who, whose, who's,* and *whom*. The word *who* is used as a subject and *whom* is used as an object. *Whose* is an adjective or pronoun that shows possession, and *who's* is a contraction for *who is*.

For example:
who: <u>Who</u> will come to the movies with me?
whom: With <u>whom</u> are you going to the movies?
whose: I don't know <u>whose</u> car you will take to the movies.
who's: Mike is the one <u>who's</u> coming to pick me up.

Complete each sentence by circling the correct word in parentheses.

1. _____ idea was it to cook spaghetti tonight? (Whose / Who's)

2. I need help from someone _____ can make meatballs. (who / whom)

3. From _____ will you get the recipe for the spaghetti sauce? (who / whom)

4. We need someone _____ not afraid to make very strong garlic bread.
(whose / who's)

5. I don't even know _____ coming to dinner. (whose / who's)

6. _____ did you invite to come tonight? (Who / Whom)

7. I don't know with _____ I will get a ride. (who / whom)

8. Let's decide _____ going to bring dessert. (whose / who's)

9. Is there anyone _____ does not like chocolate cake? (who / whom)

10. Later I will pick someone _____ going to help me clean up. (whose / who's)

My Conclusion Is...

An author does not always provide every bit of information about how a character feels or acts. The reader must **draw conclusions** about what is being read. Remember, when you draw conclusions, you use what you know to figure out something that you read.

Read the passage and answer the questions by drawing conclusions.

Rebecca could hardly contain herself as she sat on the bus going home from school. She couldn't wait to tell her parents that she was asked to have her own art show in the school auditorium. Only one student each year is asked to star in the Art in Our Auditorium show. She was elated that she was that student.

As she sat on the bus, she went through the art pieces in her mind. She would focus on abstract paintings, she thought, and maybe she would create one or two more pieces just for the show. Then she thought about what she would write in her artists' statement.

1. How do you think Rebecca feels about art? What clues from the story helped you to make your decision?

_____

_____

_____

_____

2. Why do you think the school picks only one artist per year to showcase in the auditorium?

_____

_____

_____

_____

Cause or Effect, Effect or Cause

When you read, look for cause-and-effect relationships. This can help you understand a passage better. Remember: A **cause** is a reason that something happens. An **effect** is the thing that happens as a result.

Read the passage and list causes and effects in the chart below.

Even before the invention of the telescope, people could look into the night sky and be amazed by the countless number of stars sparkling above them. They could see constellations and observe their movement during one night and throughout one year.

However, the telescope allowed for something much more impressive. When we look through a telescope, we are brought much closer to an amazing world of astronomy. The telescope has allowed us to see details of space that we cannot see with the human eye. As a result, scientists now have evidence to prove or disprove theories made in the past. We can also form new theories based on observations of the night sky. As telescopes improve in quality, we will be able to learn more and more about stars and other objects in the night sky.

Cause	Effect

What Does That Idiom Mean?

An **idiom** is a group of words that has a unique meaning that cannot be determined from the individual words.

For example:
a drop in the bucket   a tiny part of something larger
racing against the clock   running out of time to do something

Read each sentence. Write the meaning of the underlined idiom on the line.

1. Our team has never won against the Cubs, so <u>keep your fingers crossed</u>.

_____

2. This time I hope we can give the other team <u>a taste of its own medicine</u>.

_____

3. Coach would <u>bend over backwards</u> to help us win a game.

_____

4. The Cubs wear uniforms that look like they <u>cost an arm and a leg</u>.

_____

5. Coach said we should <u>go out on a limb</u> and do our very best.

_____

6. We already had a great season, so winning this game would be <u>icing on the cake</u>.

_____

7. The team is <u>on pins and needles</u> as Jack goes up to bat.

_____

8. His confidence is <u>over the top</u>, and he bats one out of the park.

_____

It's All About the Clause

A **dependent clause** is a group of words with a subject and verb that does not make a complete sentence and must be attached to another part of a sentence in order to make sense. An **independent clause** is a group of words with a subject and verb that makes a complete sentence on its own.

For example:
Dependent clause: So that we can go home.
Independent clause: Maggie will finish quickly so that we can go home.

Read each group of words. What kind of clause do the words make up?
Write *dependent* or *independent*.

1. Playing his favorite video game. _____

2. He is only allowed to play on the weekends. _____

3. Because of his homework. _____

4. He has more than an hour of homework every night. _____

5. Time seems to fly when he is playing his video games. _____

6. At his friend's house. _____

7. They can play video games together if they do their homework.
_____

8. Mom says it's OK! _____

9. Let's play. _____

10. After she shows me how to do those math problems. _____

The Right Choice, or the Write Choice?

A **homophone** is a pair or group of words that sound the same but have different meanings and spellings. The correct homophone must be used for a sentence to make sense.

Complete each sentence. Circle the correct homophone in parentheses.

1. The tailor fixed the (seam / seem) on Pedro's pants.

2. Jake was the (air / heir) who would take over the family business.

3. The librarian made sure no books were (band / banned) from her library.

4. The police would not allow people to use (guerilla / gorilla) tactics to enforce the law.

5. We will (wait / weight) for you outside on the park bench.

6. Nana (bruise / brews) the best iced tea in the neighborhood.

7. We will (canvas / canvass) the neighborhood looking for the lost dog.

8. (Whose / Who's) turn is it to take the garbage out?

9. Her painting was the most beautiful (sight / site) I had seen all day.

10. When I make it (threw / through) this book, I'll lend it to you.

11. He heard the dog (whale / wail) all night long.

12. I cleaned the bathroom because we are expecting a (guessed / guest).

Answer Key

Page 4
1. Laura and Alexander went to the movies on Jay Street yesterday.
2. Alexander could not believe his Christmas holiday was almost over.
3. He knew that it was almost time for Aunt Sarah to drive him to the Albany airport.
4. He missed his mom and dad back home, and he even missed his dog, Tootsie.
5. Next Christmas break, Alexander wants to visit Washington, D.C., or Austin, Texas.
6. He gets to choose where he visits each year with his cousin, Laura.
7. This year he went to Laura's hometown to see her in a stage production of *Annie*.
8. Aunt Sarah took them to dinner at Millie's Diner after the show.
9. Alexander ordered eggnog because it was the December holiday.
10. Eggnog reminds Alexander of being at home in New Hampshire.

Page 5
1. Jackson will have to reorganize his bookshelf.
2. Dave is impatient and does not want to wait for his friend.
3. The boys were supposed to recheck their math homework.
4. The time they spent in school studying had been unhelpful.
5. Any time for study is imperfect in some way, they thought.
6. not fulfilled
7. before destiny, or decided ahead of time
8. beyond ordinary
9. to take back, or possess again
10. after writing

Page 6
1. ment
2. ation
3. al
4. ful
5. ent
6. tion
7. philosopher
8. development
9. agreement
10. humorless

Page 7
1. should've
2. didn't
3. she'll
4. could've; didn't
5. They will; it is
6. I am; Let us
7. You will; you are
8. Would not; we will

Page 8
Friendly letters will vary.

Page 9
Synonyms may vary.
1. gorgeous; beautiful
2. smallest; tiniest
3. powerful; strong
4. excess; extra
5. most impressive; best
6. most important; greatest
7. eager; excited
8. successful; triumphant

Page 10
1. My tennis racket is somewhere.
2. You should go check out in the garage.
3. You should come to practice with us.
4. You and Michael are leaving.
5. We should leave in 10 minutes.
6. We should go.
7. We should order dinner.

Page 11
1. Andrew mowed the lawn and raked the leaves.
2. The man who lives across the street has two dogs.
3. He takes them for a walk without their leashes.
4. Neighbors up and down the block complain.
5. "Get those dogs off my lawn!" they say.
6. children
7. teeth
8. cacti or cactuses
9. halves
10. lives

Page 12
Detailed descriptions will vary.

Page 13
Possible answers:
1. preview
2. postscript
3. uncover
4. overcooked
5. impatient
6. export
7. inexperienced; without experience
8. interpersonal; between people
9. overemphasizing; emphasizing too much
10. reschedule; schedule again

Page 14
Possible answers:
1. running
2. workable
3. fruitful
4. creation
5. naturalism
6. scientist
7. doubtful; full of doubt
8. professional; one who is engaged in a profession
9. calmly; full of calm
10. determination; state of being determined

Page 15
Possible answers:
1. discouraged
2. pretty
3. rough
4. first
5. wonderfully
6. easy
7. shy; outgoing
8. inventive; unoriginal
9. appetizing; unpleasant
10. welcoming; mean

Page 16
1. past
2. future
3. present
4–6. Sentences will vary.
7. Each guest will put his or her gift on the table.
8. The kids will play party games and eat snacks.
9. Parents will pick up their children at 3:00 PM sharp.

Page 17
Topics and paragraphs will vary.

Page 18
Drafts and final copies will vary.

Page 19
1. *Mrs. Frisby and the Rats of Nimh*
2. *The Wall Street Journal*
3. *Dancing with the Stars*
4. "The Itsy-Bitsy Spider"
5. *Star Wars*
6. *The Philadelphia Inquirer*
7. "How to Make the Best Enchilada"
8. *Harry Potter and the Deathly Hallows*
9. "Helping at the Main Street Soup Kitchen"
10. *Sports Illustrated for Kids*

Page 20
1. Both use initials instead of their first names; both wrote novels for children; both were born in July; both had first books that became very popular.
2. White's books did not become popular right away but Rowling's did; White was born with the initials E.B., but Rowling was not born with the initials J.K.; White's books were not a series, but Rowling's were; White was born in the 1800s and Rowling was born in the 1960s.

Page 21
1. It; Thursday
2. They; storekeepers
3. She; Your mom
4. They; turkey, stuffing, and gravy
5. We; My family
6. We; my sister and I
7. She; Your mom
8. We; my sister and I

Page 22
Paragraphs will vary.

Page 23
1. replies
2. wish
3. have
4. changes
5. My dog is the silliest dog on my street. Whenever we go for a walk, he barks at the third house on the right, number 32. There is never anyone outside the house when he barks, and there usually aren't even any cars in the driveway. But he barks and barks until we pass it and it's far out of our sight. Maybe next time we will walk the other way to avoid this problem.

Page 24
1. games
2. grilling contest
3. a raffle drawing
4. 1. games 2. grilling contest, 3. talent contests 4. raffle drawings

Page 25
1. him; object pronoun
2. We; subject pronoun
3. They; subject pronoun
4. them; object pronoun
5. she; subject pronoun
6. them; object pronoun
7. me; object pronoun

8. us; object pronoun
9. we; subject pronoun

Page 26
1. My mom doesn't think I'm old enough to be a babysitter.
2. "I sure am!" I said excitedly.
3. "I used to take care of many babies in our neighborhood," I reminded her.
4. Everyone can use a little spare change, and I think I could use some babysitting money to use when I go to the movies with my friends. Wouldn't you agree?
5. There is a girl down the street named Whitney who is easy to babysit for.
6. "Would you like to come meet her with me?" I asked Mom.
7. "Well," said Mom. "Maybe it's not such a bad idea after all if you start babysitting."

Page 27
1. Pam does not want anybody to get hurt on the new playground.
2. She won't let the crews put up swing sets that are dangerous.
3. Nothing will stop her from doing the job right.
4. An unsafe playground isn't fun for anybody.
5. The workers will draw a line in front of the swings so no one will get hit.
6. Better grip handles will be put on the monkey bars so little hands won't ever slip.
7. There won't be anywhere in town with such a safe playground.

Page 28
1. I am wearing a (raincoat) with a hood because the weather report calls for rain.
2. Jackie saw a (line) of fifty people waiting to get into the parade area.
3. This will be a (parade) of great importance for our baseball league.
4. (Players) from every team will be here.
5. We're celebrating the (teams) with the best sportsmanship.
6. (Everyone) in the parade should be proud.
7. My dad will be (one) of the people on the sidelines.
8. My mom will be (one) of the volunteers in the float.
9. I have a whole (family) of great supporters.

Page 29
Story beginnings will vary.

Page 30
1. some; plural
2. Many; plural
3. Nobody; singular
4. Everybody; singular
5. Few; plural
6. rings
7. comes
8. want
9. is
10. sighs

Page 31
1. opens
2. want
3. look
4. reach
5. want
6. like
7. see
8. surprises
9. opens
10. think

Page 32
Narratives will vary.

Page 33
1. condition
2. ordinary
3. consider
4. popular
5. science
6. alphabet
7. medicate
Possible answers:
8. discussion
9. finalize
10. absolutely
11. energize
12. refill
13. rewrite
14. pharmacist

Page 34
1. colder; comparative
2. sweetest; superlative
3. older; comparative
4. smoother; comparative
5. sunniest; superlative
6. laziest; superlative
7. best; superlative
8. funniest; superlative

Page 35
Jackson has always been obsessed with tigers. Ever since he was a little boy, he has been asking his parents for tiger print wallpaper for his room. He has six stuffed animals of tigers and 12 books about tigers and their habitats, eating habits, and adaptations. He has been to the local zoo about once a month to visit the tigers there. He has come to know them all by name. Jackson's mom thinks that he should write to the zoo to ask for a special zoo tour.
1. There is a new park being built on Rayborne Avenue.

2. My older brother is one of the construction workers on the site.
3. He says it's going to be the best park around town because it has a hedge maze.

Page 36
1. The polling places in town have been too crowded and people walk away without voting.
2. He wants the mayor to add more polling volunteers.
3. He thinks the plan will work because more volunteers will be able to help more voters and help things run more smoothly.

Page 37
Effects will vary.

Page 38
1. Dad raced us toward the parking lot, but we were five minutes late. Dad raced us toward the parking lot. We were five minutes late.
2. After dropping us off, he went to the parent area, and we took our bikes to the starting line. After dropping us off, he went to the parent area. We took our bikes to the starting line.
3. The race official quickly handed us our numbers, and Sara needed help to put hers on. The race official quickly handed us our numbers. Sara needed help to put hers on.
4. I was nervous to see all of the other bikers standing at the starting line, and it would be a few more minutes until I was ready. I was nervous to see all of the other bikers standing at the starting line. It would be a few more minutes until I was ready.
5. "One minute until the starting gun goes off," said the official as my heart began racing even faster. "One minute until the starting gun goes off," said the official. My heart began racing even faster.

Page 39
Possible answers:
1. You're up so late tonight, so it's time to get some sleep.
2. I know that is a really good book, but you have to put it down now.
3. I'm going to turn off the light now, so don't get startled.
4. We can go to the beach tomorrow, so you can bring the book with you.
5. During the American Revolution, colonists became

free from England (and) we drafted our own constitution.
6. George Washington led the colonial army, (but) Thomas Jefferson had the role of writing the Declaration of Independence.
7. In the Civil War, the northern and southern states fought each other, (and) some families were divided as a result.
8. States from the South were called the Confederacy, (and) states from the North were called the Union.

Page 40
Concept maps will vary.

Page 41
1. Ashley has been eating the cereal each morning.
2. Ashley was able to ask for more cereal.
3. The cereal is healthy and tastes good.

Page 42
Interview questions will vary.

Page 43
Articles will vary.

Page 44
Paragraphs will vary.

Page 45
1. cashier
2. ripe
3. line
4. grocery list
5. grocery cart
6. snacks

Page 46
1. complete
2. incomplete; There are many species of polar bears.
3. complete
4. complete
5. complete
6. incomplete; Polar bears live among icy habitats in ocean environments.

Page 47
2, 6, 3, 1, 4, 5

Page 48
Sentences will vary.

Page 49
Story middles will vary.

Page 50
1. We laugh at his jokes (and) listen to the tape again.
2. Josh wants to be a comedian (and) writes his own jokes.
3. His mom takes him to auditions (and) waits for him in the car.

4. She hears laughter coming from inside the auditorium, and smiles.
5. Josh's mom sticks with her kids and helps them when they need it.
6. Josh came out of the auditorium smiling and walked to the car.
7. He felt like he had just won a million bucks and acted like it, too.
8. His mom called out from the car and cheered for him.
9. Josh thanked all of his friends for helping him, but thanked his mom first.

Page 51
"I love to sing," I told Julio. "But I don't think I can sing in front of an audience."
Julio answered, "Just pretend the audience is not there. Don't think about them and you can concentrate on singing."
I told Julio what I thought. "I have tried all sorts of tricks," I told him. "Nothing works. I would much rather just play my guitar and not worry about singing."
"Alright," he said, "but if you change your mind, there is an opening in our band for a rock star!"

Page 52
Brainstorming lists and paragraphs will vary.

Page 53
1. The author thinks multiplication should be learned as repeated addition.
2. The author thinks memorization does not teach the student how to truly understand multiplication.
3. Viewpoints will vary.

Page 54
1. secretary's
2. farmer's
3. physicist's
4. airport's
5. eggplant's
6. family's
7. essay's
8. uncle's
9. president's
10. Larry's
11. onions'
12. mice's
13. candies'
14. coats'
15. parachutes'
16. people's
17. balloons'
18. sweaters'
19. janitors'
20. companies'

21. the dog's treat
22. the car's wheels
23. the book's pages
24. the students' efforts
25. the stores' parking spots

Page 55
1. comparative
2. superlative
3. comparative
4. comparative
5. comparative
6. superlative
7. superlative
8. comparative
9. superlative
10. comparative
11. comparative
12. superlative
13. Jessica's class is quietest.
14. Ravi's car is the least expensive to fill with gas.
15. The first play was the most entertaining.

Page 56
Sentences will vary.
1. cautiously
2. outside
3. playfully
4. patiently
5. nervously
6. very; here
7. loudly
8. maybe; quickly

Page 57
Descriptions will vary.

Page 58
Facts: The telephone was invented in 1876 by Alexander Graham Bell. Networks of telephone lines expanded through the country. People used the phone to keep in touch and do business.
In the 1940s, technology for cell phones was invented.
Opinions: People loved the new technology of the telephone.
The first cell phones were difficult to use and did not sound good.
The cell phones we use today are revolutionary. Cell phones have changed our lives for the better.

Page 59
Possible Sentences:
1. My sister is rooting around in her purse.
2. The lawyer gave the woman a contract to sign.
3. Today we will polish the silver for Grandma.
4. The baby will sometimes refuse to take his bottle.
5. The desert is usually very hot and dry.
6. The loggers used their axes to cut down the trees.

7. When you move, your address changes.
8. We can row across the lake.

Page 60
Short stories will vary.

Page 61
1. secretive
2. supplies
3. continued
4. wonder
5. barking
6. impatient
7. mean
8. boring
9. destroy
10. angered

Page 62
Sentences will vary.
1. into the woods.
2. in the strange environment.
3. in the history books.
4. to Cat's house.
5. with goodies from Cat's refrigerator.
6. to the woods with a smile on his face.
7. with me; to you.
8. near the stream; on a log.

Page 63
Venn Diagrams will vary.

Page 64
How–to articles will vary.

Page 65
Possible conclusions:
1. Animals are mammals and they have the same characteristics as the rest of the animals in that group.
2. They may have an instinct to protect their children and keep them safe from harm.
3. Human babies rely more heavily on their parents to survive than other animals.
4. Bear cubs are similar to human babies in some ways.

Page 66
Poems will vary.

Page 67
1. fact
2. fact
3. opinion
4. fact
5. opinion
6. opinion

Page 68
Answers will vary.

Page 69
Conclusions will vary.

Page 70
Persuasive letters will vary.

Page 71
1. beautifully; played the flute
2. hard; hours
3. quiet; audience
4. wildly; people cheer
5. approving; glance
6. nervous; Sabrina
7. handsomely; perform
8. politely; smiled
9. stunning; bouquet of flowers

Page 72
Plots will vary.

Page 73
Expository paragraphs will vary.

Page 74
Stories will vary.

Page 75
Possible revised version:
Namita bit into the granola bar and started chewing. Ow, she thought to herself. "Why does that tooth bother me every time I eat?" she asked herself. She hated going to the dentist, but she was lucky enough to never have had a cavity. Now she wondered if her luck had run out and if this is what a cavity feels like. She put the granola bar down and went to talk to her mom. "I need to see the dentist," she said sadly.

Page 76
Venn diagrams will vary.

Page 77
Narratives will vary.

Page 78
1. our
2. them
3. us
4. me
5. their
6. The train picked up the eager passengers and their heavy luggage.
7. The last stop on the train route is theirs.
8. One of the first stops on the train is mine.
9. Which stop is yours?

Page 79
1. The community center offers field trips, picnics, movie nights, and holiday gatherings.
2. Next week, Theresa, Paco, Jorge, and Jay are organizing an event in honor of Veterans Day.
3. They may not have enough volunteers, but they will continue with their planning anyway.

4. They are asking guests to bring various cakes, cookies, brownies, and other baked goods.
5. People should know, however, that there will be no refrigerator available for people to store food.
6. First, they will hang posters in the community center to advertise the event.
7. Then, they will hang similar posters in the park, local schools, and along Main Street.
8. They wanted to put an advertisement in the newspaper, but they did not have a budget for it.
9. Events at the community center always have a good turnout, so they are pretty sure that there will be a lot of people to enjoy the event with them.
10. My mom, dad, grandmother, and uncle will be at the event; however, they heard there will be rain that day.

Page 80
1. April commented on the plots of the books.
2. The series is a favorite of my friends.
3. We like to see them on the shelves of libraries.
4. The family reunion was the cousins' idea.
5. They sent out the uncles' invitations.
6. We asked for the families' recipes.
7. Some people were unhappy with the songs' volume.

Page 81
1. among
2. weather
3. complement
4. except
5. advice
6. lend
7. allot
8. beside
9. aside
10. effects

Page 82
1. bold
2. convince to join
3. habit
4. with hidden difficulties
5. everyone agrees
6. is a symbol of
7. done with difficulty
8. make return

Page 83
1. reintroduction
2. miscommunication
3. unnecessarily
4. reviewing
5. one who

6. one who
7. to do again
8. in combination with
9. out or outside
10. able to

Page 84
1. simile
2. alliteration
3. metaphor
4. onomatopoeia
5. alliteration
6. metaphor
7. metaphor
8. onomatopoeia
9. simile
10. alliteration

Page 85
Main idea: Colin was excited to test a new video game.
Supporting details may vary.

Page 86
1. Whose
2. who
3. whom
4. who's
5. who's
6. Who
7. whom
8. who's
9. who
10. who's

Page 87
Possible answers:
1. Rebecca feels passionate about art. I can tell because she is so happy to be chosen as the artist for the auditorium show. She was also excited to pick the art that she would display.
2. The school probably wants to reward one artist for doing so well and allow people to learn a lot about and focus on the artist.

Page 88

Cause	Effect
People have always loved to look at the night sky.	The invention of the telescope was impressive to many people who wanted to view the night sky.
The telescope allowed for more detailed views of the night sky.	Scientists could prove or disprove theories about the night sky.
Telescopes improved in quality.	We could learn even more about the objects in the night sky.

Page 89
1. wish us luck
2. do to them what they normally do to us
3. do anything possible
4. were very expensive
5. do more than you normally would

6. above and beyond what is expected
7. very nervous
8. extreme

Page 90
1. dependent
2. independent
3. dependent
4. independent
5. independent
6. dependent
7. independent
8. independent
9. independent
10. dependent

Page 91
1. seam
2. heir
3. banned
4. guerilla
5. wait
6. brews
7. canvass
8. Whose
9. sight
10. through
11. wail
12. guest